CHANEL

First published in Great Britain in 1996 by
Thames and Hudson Ltd, London

British Library Cataloguing-in-Publication Data

A catalogue record for this book is available from the British Library

ISBN 0-500-01720-4

Printed and bound in Italy

CHANEL

TEXT BY FRANÇOIS BAUDOT

THAMES AND HUDSON

1

ike a tale from *The Arabian Nights*, Chanel's life story is one of magical transformations. She had five distinct lives (five being without a doubt her lucky number), and while each one does not spring directly from the one before, they were nevertheless connected by one continuous thread which stretched from the beginning of this century to the end: style. The Chanel look was to survive all the changing dictates of fashion. Its principles were order, poise and good taste, as distinct from 'tastefulness'.

Chanel No. 1 came into the world by accident on 19 August 1883 in Saumur. Her father was a pedlar; her mother, a peasant woman, died young. With no identity papers to bear witness to her beginnings, the origins of this very first Chanel, Gabrielle Chanel, remain shrouded in mystery. She attended a convent in Aubazine where she was made to wear black by the nuns. Under these echoing Cistercian vaults she plied her needle and learned the ways of silence: austerity, good manners and solitude. Aubazine, in Corrèze, was still in the Middle Ages but the twentieth century was knocking at the door.

C hanel No. 2 started out in Moulins, a garrison town, where she sang in bars known as *café-concerts* and became known as Coco. Slight and dark, with jet black eyes, a triangular feline face and an equine nose, the young girl already stood out from the other singers around her. Now she gained a name for herself – and admirers. Some of these were wealthy, some were titled, often they were both, and they wanted fun – with a different sort of woman. Coco was twenty-five years old. She had a good figure and she wanted to get out of her situation. What other option was there? She went to live with a man called Etienne Balsan in the outskirts of Paris. He was a man of the world, an anti-snob who respected her at least as much as the thoroughbreds that he admired so passionately. Chanel's second incarnation was inextricably bound up with horses; the austere elegance and the almost militaristic streamlining of the riding habit made a lasting impression on her. In the saddle she learned an essential discipline: never to use force but always to remain relaxed. Both the *haute école* and *haute couture* as practised by Chanel share this understated elegance, this valuing of discretion over ostentation. Chanel would go on to teach it to her followers. Who better than Gabrielle to observe this very masculine, very English principle, keeping company as she did then with wealthy sporting types? One of them, Boy Capel, more handsome and more brilliant than any of the others, became her lover and, more importantly, her friend. (He died young and came to symbolize for her a passion that would remain forever unfulfilled.) Capel soon realized that the only thing the wise and beautiful Coco really loved was work – and not the kind of work she had done hitherto. What the young woman wanted was to use her hands, her head and her very definite likes and dislikes. And so it was decided: Chanel would be a milliner. It was her road to freedom.

etienne Balsan generously offered her his ground floor bachelor flat, which Coco transformed into a studio. Her girlfriends, who were still leading the good life with their various gentleman admirers, wore her first creations, thinking they were doing her a favour. Sometimes she was mocked for her boaters decorated with just one knot of big black beads, or for her stylish schoolgirl dresses but it was a changing world and Coco was on the right track. To the women of the Belle Epoque who passed each other in their glittering splendour at Maxims, tarted up in feathers and weighed down with lace and pearls, Chanel's designs seemed somewhat unsophisticated. But youth was taking over, and without fully realizing it, Chanel was inventing a concept which was destined to shape the future.

When she moved to rue Cambon in Paris in 1910, the world was ready for her. Knowing she was the right person at the right time, she opened a shop at number 21. Crowds flocked to it, and in a matter of just a few years, she took over numbers 27, 29 and 31 of the same street; her original fashion house there still carries her name. After the war, haute couture was to become a major industry, catering for an affluent bourgeois clientele just as expensive ready-to-wear clothes shops do today. Chanel became the object of bitter rivalries, internecine feuding and high financial stakes. The young woman was ready for them and would win. In her ivory tower she owned an apartment where she never slept. Above it was the workshop which she rarely left. On the beige door can still be read the imperious, timeless, anonymous 'Mademoiselle'. Written in black letters, it signalled the end of a long journey.

It was now time for Chanel No. 3 to be born. Not entirely by chance the place where she was to blossom, to grow and to come into her own was one that combined sea, horses and men: Deauville on the north French coast. A few months before the First World War broke out, she opened a boutique there with 'Gabrielle Chanel' emblazoned on the awning. As well as her extremely minimal hats, the young milliner had already begun making a few discreet accessories inspired by workmen's and sailors' clothes. Her easy-fitting, flowing designs could be worn for exercise and for sport. They were made for a kind of woman who so far only existed in the mind of their creator. Chanel preferred getting a sun-tan exercising in the fresh air and bathing in the sea, to perspiring in ostentatious dresses at balls and casinos in spa towns. She was a privileged partner of men, rubbing shoulders with them as an equal. Soon she was to prove that she could surpass them.

Slight, androgynous and sun-tanned, Coco would plunder the wardrobe of the poor for ideas. She wore a college girl's gabardine raincoat or a fisherman's outfit in white twill, dark wool and chiné jersey. Her skirts were short, so that she could the more quickly run up the ladder of fashion. Nobody realized that she was inventing the style of Chanel, the elegance of Chanel, the age of Chanel. Picasso had just painted *Les Demoiselles d'Avignon*. Stravinsky had composed *The Rite of Spring*. Diaghilev was starting his Ballets Russes. Who would have guessed that one day all of them would be her friends? Of those who smiled condescendingly at this slim woman, always plainly dressed and alone, how many would have foreseen that the ostentatious reticence, the ruinously expensive simplicity and the gilded poverty that she was introducing, would become the subtlest, most powerful kind of élitism which would determine what women wore and how they behaved for the next fifty years?

meanwhile the privileged classes were starting to grumble. Income tax was beginning to bite. Women had become emancipated. During the war they had replaced men in the factories, and to stop their plaits getting caught in the machinery, they cut their hair short. Society itself was increasingly industrial; speed, not sport, was the new leisure activity. Racing cars flashed by, aeroplanes soared, steamers cut through the waves. And the epitome of this 'new man in a hurry' was Boy Capel. The love, the life and the financial backer of the young milliner was the very antithesis of the old-style idle Parisian gentleman strolling along the boulevards and the banks of the Seine. Brought up in England, he had made his fortune selling coal for the railways to wartime France. He was to be killed at the wheel of his sportscar.

Just as the oyster's irritation secretes the pearl, so Coco came out of this ordeal all the stronger, wrenching open her shell to face her solitude once more. Even in its depths, she was polishing up her best weapons ready for the battle ahead. This time the third Chanel got it right. She carefully blotted out her past as a poor orphan, music-hall singer and the demi-mondaine that she almost became, discarding (as she did in her biography) an entire decade from her life. In her own creations, she even looked ten years younger.

Withdrawing herself (and therefore making herself all the more sought after), Chanel No. 3 gave up all hope of happiness again, and resigned herself to a life of plots and business deals. Yet shy and unsure of her powers as she was, she enchanted Paris during *les années folles*. Who would have predicted the impact that her temperament and her creations were about to have?

Coco still knew only a handful of the polo playing set and had everything to learn about the world on which she was already sitting in judgment. It was Misia Sert, a sort of *fin-de-siècle* muse, who was to help her break into the Parisian scene. First she met Jean Cocteau, Raymond Radiguet, Les Six and the *Boeuf sur le Toit* gang. Then it was Serge Lifar, Christian Bérard, José Maria Sert, Blaise Cendrars, Pierre Reverdy, Salvador Dalí, the Bourdets, the Beaumonts, the Jouhandeaus ... All those who had swept away the past with the creation of modern art were to meet the woman who had buried Worth, outshone Paquin and killed off the great Paul Poiret; she who had freed women's bodies from tight-lacing corsets and padding, restoring them to their natural state; who was responsible for Egyptian dancers, Ancient Greek shepherdesses and wild children roaming the countryside in schoolgirl smocks. Chanel was the dark side of Colette; more of a Jeanne with her dry bread than the schoolgirl Claudine. The two women sized each other up, appraised each other and showed, each in her own way, how it was possible to be feminine while turning one's back on class. Thousands of women now began to realize that 'poor chic' could be the answer to social snobbery. The Chanel look, with its lines reduced to their simplest expression, shows that *how* clothes are worn is much more important than *what* is worn; that a good line is worth more than a pretty face; that well-dressed is not the same as dressy, and that the acme of social cachet was to be proletarian. Youth, according to Chanel, should not have to declare itself, it should be obvious all the time: in sitting down, getting into a car, walking down the street, stretching out a leg or raising an arm. It was about ideals rather than outfits, concepts rather then costumes. What has made her style last is the fact that it is functional, which is in keeping with the pace of contemporary life.

But in addition to this, it was the audacity with which she used herself as the model for her own creations that allowed Chanel from the thirties onwards to impose her ideas on fashion. 'I invented sportswear for myself,' as she would later say. 'I set the fashion for the very reason that I was the first twentieth-century woman.' Before Chanel, the fashion designer was merely a supplier. Chanel raised herself to the rank of her clients, whom she would always refuse to meet. What she did do was to enlist some of them into her fashion house and her business. Princesses displayed her dresses and sold her jewelry, designed by other penniless aristocrats who were duly paid. By being the one who did the paying, was the boarder from the orphanage buying her freedom? From now on it was the fashion designers who threw the balls and the upper crust who anxiously fished for invitations.

●

'I am a lie that tells the truth'; that paradox of Jean Cocteau could have been embossed on the cover of Coco Chanel's life story. Under the influence of the men in her life, she enriched a style which was essentially her own. The exiled Grand Duke Dmitri of Russia, a relation of Tsar Nicholas II, introduced Chanel, the daughter of the street pedlar from the Auvergne, to the splendour of Byzantine imperial icons and baroque jewelry, which inspired her. She then scattered sparkling imitations over her little usherette dresses. 'A woman's décolleté is not just a container for jewellery', she said, but this was in fact not quite true of her own. For example, she audaciously wore pearls with a tweed jacket while riding with the Duke of Westminster. He shared her life for ten years, during which time she learned the power of great wealth and also the detachment, distance and isolation that a great name can bring. 'Westminster is elegance itself. He never has anything new – I had to go and buy him some shoes. He has been wearing the same jackets for twenty-five years'. Today such comments seem pure Chanel. She ended her description with wry humour: 'It's just as bad being too rich as it is being too tall. In the first case, you can't find happiness and in the second, you can't find a bed'. Towards the end of her life, such aphorisms were characteristic of Coco's wit. She had developed a taste for them while she was still young through her association with a remarkable poet, Pierre Reverdy, an innovator and precursor of the Cubists, to whom she gave lasting friendship and support. This great mystic had wit enough and to spare, and Chanel made good use of him. At odd moments, she would write maxims that her friend would correct or complete; for this he was tactfully renumerated. 'He who pays his debts gets richer,' she once said with her proletarian common sense to the Tsarina. She also spent an enormous amount of money on Paul Iribe. When she met him at the beginning of the thirties, she was at the peak of her glory. A creative yet also strangely destructive individual, Iribe was a remarkable illustrator, and a designer of furniture, jewelry and interior decorations. He collaborated with Paul Poiret, Jean Cocteau and various Hollywood film-makers, artists often more talented than himself. He was the classic type of artistic director. It has been suggested that during their affair he made some contribution to his mistress's style, for instance in the collection of jewelry made entirely out of soft platinum and diamonds of the first water which she launched in 1932 (the comets and carbuncles have since been re-created by the jewelry department of Chanel).

It eventually became clear that Mademoiselle Chanel had no intention of providing the Duke of Westminster with his much desired heir, and at the age of forty-five, he got married and had children with someone else. Europe meanwhile was in crisis and heading towards war, and Coco was seriously thinking of marrying Paul Iribe. She was fifty years old but looked thirty. Her picture would be taken by the greatest fashion photographers in the world including Man Ray, Horst P. Horst and George Hoyningen-Huene. In her the role of the model was crystallizing into that of role model – a model with personality, a model who could talk. This concept was realized remarkably enough in the eighties when Inès de la Fressange, 'the face of Chanel', would launch the reign of the supermodel.

What gave Chanel her image was the logo (not as yet called this): the letters, the typography, the gold, the black and the white; the use of repetition, which anticipated Pop Art; the perfecting of a grammar and a vocabulary which belonged to her alone; the expression of her masculine side and her intense femininity; her brown, angular, suntanned figure, and her lack of sentimentality. From Mademoiselle through Gabrielle to Coco, then finally becoming Chanel, she had pulled herself up to join the highest ranks of fashion personalities. More than that, she was one of the chosen few who shaped an entire era when everything was being reinvented. In 1938 Picasso painted *Guernica*. Michel Leiris wrote prophetically regarding this painting: 'All that we love is going to die.' Paul Iribe had already suffered a fatal heart attack after a game of tennis at Chanel's villa in the south of France. Once again she was left to her splendid isolation. Rich, famous and at times wearied by devastating setbacks, she closed her fashion house in 1939. 'I thought there wouldn't be any more dresses,' she explained pathetically. A page had been turned, and the story could have ended there.

'**m**any of Chanel's private dicta have entered into the unspoken rules that still govern fashion', wrote Cecil Beaton, an expert on the matter, in *The Glass of Fashion*, a treatise on good manners and thus also on good dress sense in the twentieth century. Writing at the beginning of the fifties, the photographer continued: 'After the war Chanel retired from the active world of fashion,' and he concludes with great foresight: 'Though Chanel herself echoed the theory that fashions are never revived, it is a tribute to her rare and remarkable practicality, and an anomaly in the annals of recorded fashion, that few of her innovations became dated. With each season she watched, like Nature's seeds, her past creativity flowering anew, barely hidden behind the vague alterations of less talented designers.' He chose his words carefully.

During the deep sleep of the Occupation years Chanel champed at the bit. A handsome German would meet her in secret at rue Cambon, filling her empty life and speaking English to her. Chanel got out of France and went to Switzerland. She stayed there for eight long years, interspersed with short stays in Paris and the United States. It was the success of Christian Dior that hit her most hard. She who had presided over the revolution of fashion now watched from her exile the restoration of costume. Rustling petticoats, draped fabrics, wasp-waists, hems down to the ankles … Dior's 'New Look' in 1947 was the antithesis of the Chanel style. Now it was the eternal woman, a queen, a star, a pin-up, celebrating the return of prosperity in a dazzling display. After the Liberation, no one had any use for the 'little under-nourished telegraph girls' of Coco's designs. The ideal woman of the Fourth Republic was definitely well-covered.

Chanel waited and kept quiet, letting men such as Dior, Cristobal

Balenciaga, Pierre Balmain and Jacques Fath believe that once again they could be the ones in control of women's destinies. But surely women would not have forgotten the freedom Coco had promised them? The New Look came and went. In 1953 the designer, coiled up on her couch like a cobra preparing to strike, felt that Chanel's time had come round again.

Chanel No. 4 made her comeback on 5 February 1954 but to an icy reception. She was over seventy years old. A failure would not just be a terrible disappointment, it would also jeopardize the one remaining asset from her empire: her perfumes. To try her luck a second time at an age when most people have long been retired, required a great deal of self-assurance. But since her youth, Gabrielle Chanel had defiantly cheated time. She clung to her belief that: 'I set the fashion for a quarter of a century because I was of my time and it is important to do things exactly at the right moment. Fashions change but style remains.' She proved it immediately. The first collection of her second career was more than a come-back, it was a veritable rebirth. True, the French press derided her and faithful supporters were thin on the ground; Dior was still the unanimous favourite. But slowly and surely, the Chanel machinery started up once again. 'What's new? Chanel,' read the cover of *Elle* magazine. Its founder, Hélène Lazareff, who had come back from the United States in 1945 full of new ideas for women, would from now on offer unwavering support for the Chanel look in the pages of her magazine. The fashions of this famous little dressmaker now took to the streets. No imitator could ever come close to the original or to her phoenix-like ability to renew herself. This is still true nearly forty years later. The Americans were quicker than the French to realize that a real Chanel phenomenon was underway; they applauded and bought into it. From now on, they too would have their say in the fashion world. A year after her legendary comeback, the great Coco, now restored to her old reputation, reconquered the rest of her empire. Soft jackets with no interlining, wonderfully managed sleeves, silk blouses, gold chains, wrap-over skirts, quilted shoulder bags leaving the hands free, flat shoes with a bar across and a black toe to shorten the foot, jewel-like buttons on jackets and false buttons cascading down the front of the garment ... plus a thousand other original ideas which have today been eagerly adopted by the general public. The 'Chanel Look', as it was christened by the English-speaking press, swept across both sides of the Atlantic. It was a landslide victory.

t he image the public had of Chanel was of an elderly woman wearing a hat, her eyebrows pencilled in more and more heavily, arched under her dark locks, and a stern mouth, humiliating anyone who did not bow before her very upright steely figure. Or sitting on the steps of her couture house, concealed behind a forest of gold, Coromandel lacquer work and rock crystals. She was the high priestess of classicism whose judgments could not be questioned and who, right to the end, continued perfecting her profile and her style, spinning, weaving and snipping like the three Fates rolled into one. This fearsome yet magnetic image is the one that has lasted; the dressmaking queen bee who, since her return, lived at the Ritz on the other side of the Rue Cambon. Then, one Sunday in 1971, she died. That day her hive closed down. But this was not the last of her: the memory of the woman who had rejected her own past was now to enjoy a considerable afterlife.

Coco, a key-figure of her time who had fashioned herself as well as her own style, lived on in Chanel. It is a family name which, to the detriment of the house of Chanel, and in fact illegally, has become a common noun. Six letters to sum up a legend of the twentieth century, the fifth incarnation being her most enduring perfume.

Beyond a doubt, Chanel No. 5 leaves the most famous trail of scent in the world. When it was launched in 1920 from an original creation by the perfumer Ernest Beaux, it was totally novel. In its small stoppered bottle with its sharp lines, embossed with its reference number, this abstract fragrance was created from a secret cocktail of over eighty ingredients. In one day, Chanel had supplanted and killed off traditional perfume which instantly became old-fashioned. Before her, perfume was not the business of the fashion designer. Cut-glass bottles displayed names like 'Evening Revery', 'Pink Clover', 'Spray of Happiness' and other romantic names with easily identifiable flower oils. Chanel No. 5 smelled like none of these scents, nor like anything other than itself. It was sufficient to prolong Chanel's name, couture house and work well beyond her own life span.

t he fifth life of Chanel is as astonishing as the others, although much harder to tell, since it is an ongoing story. It continues with each new season and each carefully modified collection, through each new perfume and beauty product created by Chanel and stamped with the logo known the world over. After Gabrielle Chanel's death, her fashion house, her salons and her studio were dormant for a decade. This was a necessary time of mourning during which her entire empire turned in on itself and looked back to its founder to reflect on and negotiate her return to the forefront of fashion. Once again, her empire was calm, resolute and implacable.

Leaving other fashions to come and go, the Chanel look was relaunched under the leadership of Karl Lagerfeld, reconquering the magazine pages of the early eighties. To the rules and regulations of Chanel that he knew so well, the new fashion director added a slogan that he had borrowed from Goethe: 'Make a better future by developing elements from the past.' While so many couture houses died off, the name of Chanel still figures among those on the cutting edge of contemporary fashion. In fact, Karl Lagerfeld is one of the few French designers who can stand up to the invincible power of the ready-to-wear fashions from Milan. Today, fashion is no longer the exclusive privilege of Paris, but an international affair, given instant media coverage to all four corners of the globe. Upsetting Chanel's principles, juggling sometimes outrageously with her laws, practising like no one else in fashion design the art of not pleasing everyone (apart from perhaps Chanel herself), Karl Lagerfeld still knew how to introduce into each of his fashion shows for Chanel since 1983 numerous updated versions of designs formerly created by Coco. The public, however, is still able to spot a pure Chanel creation in spite of the changes, whether in Lagerfeld's haute couture or in his ready-to-wear designs.

The same continuity exists in her perfume business, where Jacques Helleu, the artisitic director, and Jacques Polge, the 'nose' of Chanel, maintain a top class tradition, as much for 'No. 5' as for the new perfumes for men and women launched by the company.

And so the new fragrance proposed by Chanel in 1996 was simply called 'Allure'. It is as though the beautiful people of today are acknowledging their debt to the everlasting elegance of Gabrielle Chanel; a woman so individual that she could claim everyone was just like her. In the history of the twentieth century, simplicity will undoubtedly be the last word in luxury.

1916
la première
robe parue
en rédactionnel

1912
au départ
un chapeau

coco
dans son
premier
tailleur
de jersey
version
1917

une
ligne
toute
nouvelle
pour
1916

les débuts de Coco
Karl Lagerfeld

Coco dans ses
robes à succès

petite robe
de 1919

la petite
robe
Ford 25

Deauville
ou
Biarritz
coco fit e

deux
modèles de
le fameuse
collection
"noire"

on l'appella
alors "la reine
du beige

tailleur
Chanel
version 1929

Les Années 20

Karl Lagerfeld

les robes du soir fennenent sa gloire alors

le camelia fait 20 apparition sous forme de bijoux

robe de dentelles 1938

coco dans une de ses célèbres robes "gitane" de 1939

1935 le sac in est encore pochette

le petit Chanel 1938 plus ceintre et épaules plus larges que 15 ans après

a la fin des années 30 le look "Coco" est en place

Karl Lagerfeld 91

Les Années 30

Le Triomphe de Coco

coco sourit... elle a bientôt 80 ans!

le sac
les bijoux
les chaussures
le camélia
les boutons
les chaînes
toi es!
toi là!!

une mode résolument
moderne basée sur une idée du passé.

La Fin des Années 50
Début des Années 60

La dame des années 50 devient une femme moderne

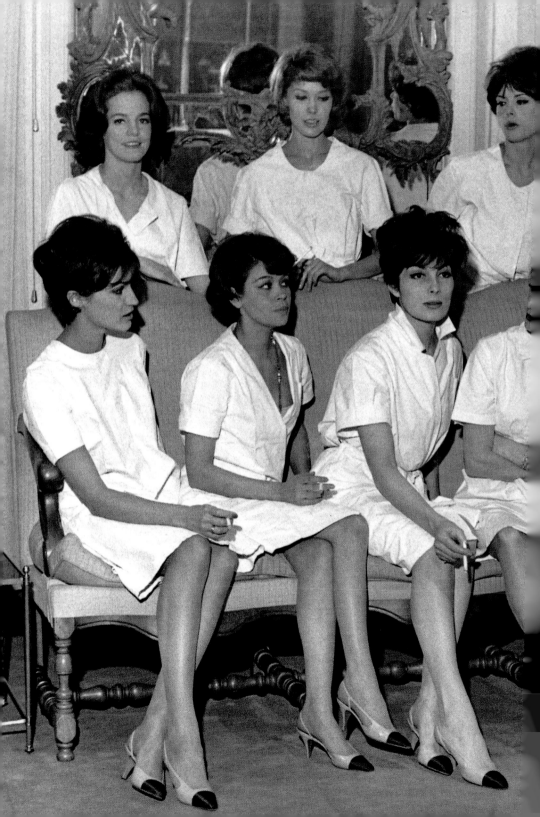

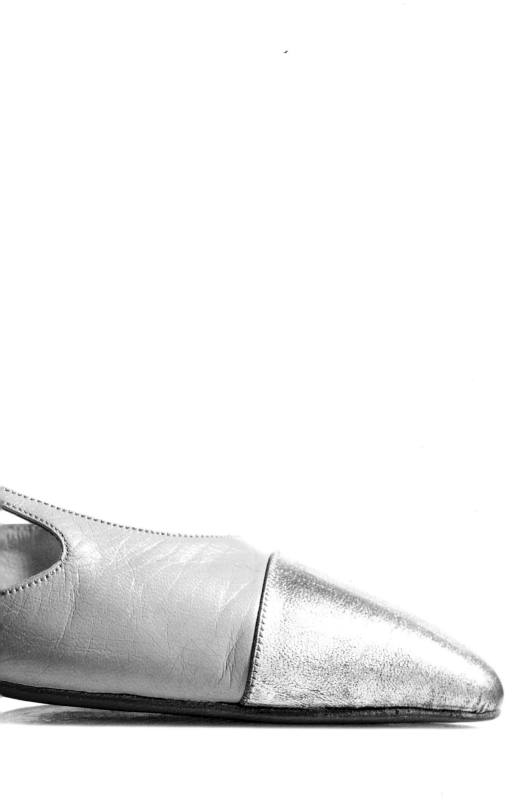

With Serge Lifar in front of her portrait by Cassandre

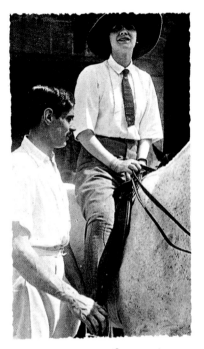

With Boy Capel

With Grand Duke Dmitri of Russia

With the Prince of Faucigny-Lucinge

With the actor Louis Jouvet and Serge Lifar

With Christian Bérard

With Salvador Dali

The poet
Pierre Reverdy

Jean Renoir
in 1940

Jean Cocteau
in 1934

The Duke of
Westminster

Paul Morand

Serge Diaghilev

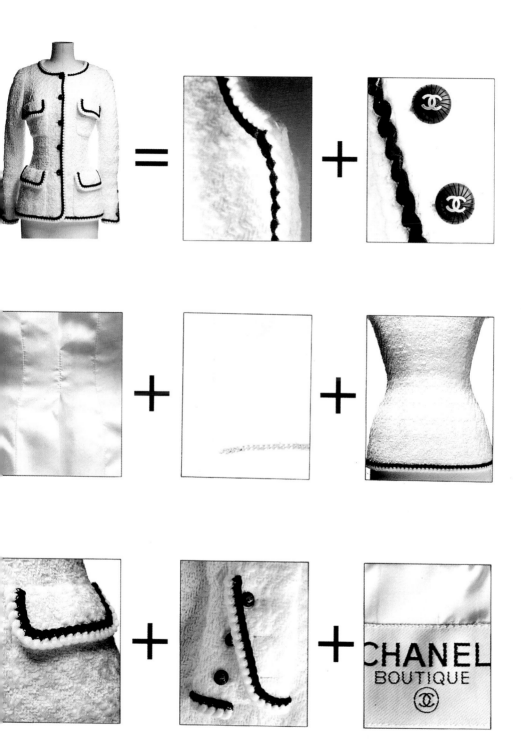

92

31

5

Not what
but how
next?

The beat
goes on....
juin 91

"Faire un meilleur avenir
"avec les éléments élargis du passé"
(Goethe)

Karl Lagerfeld 91

Select Chronology

1883   On 19 August Gabrielle Chanel is born in Saumur, France.

1910   Chanel, known from now on as Coco, sets up a hat shop at 21, rue Cambon, Paris, under the label 'Chanel Mode'. She creates a sensation at the racetrack in Longchamp with her simple tailored suit, in marked contrast to the over-elaborate finery of the day.

1913   Opens her first fashion boutique in Deauville.

1915   Opens a couture house in Biarritz.

1916   Introduces jersey. Her first published design appears in *Harper's Bazaar* accompanied by the caption 'the charming chemise dress'.

1921   Opening of 31, rue Cambon.
Launch of the first Chanel perfume: the famous 'No. 5'.
'No. 22' is launched in 1922, followed by 'Gardénia' (1925), 'Bois des Iles' (1926), 'Cuir de Russie' (1927), 'Sycomore' and 'Une Idée' (1930) and 'Jasmin' (1932).

1924   The Chanel Perfume company is set up.

1926   Introduces 'the little black dress'.

1928   Moves into rue Cambon where the avant-garde décor combines purity and unity of style. Introduces tweed. Her first suits are made from tweed specially woven for her in Scotland.

1929   Accessories boutique set up inside the couture house.

1930   Signs contract with Samuel Goldwyn to dress the stars of United Artists.

1931   Designs the dresses worn by Gloria Swanson in *Tonight or Never*; the first film on which she collaborated.

1934   Sets up a specialist workshop to develop her range of elaborate costume jewelry with the help of Count Étienne de Beaumont and Duke Fulco di Verdura. Starts a fashion for long gilt chains and for mixing different coloured gems.

1935   Chanel is at the height of her success, employing nearly 4,000 workers and selling close to 28,000 designs a year all over the world.

1939   Outbreak of the Second World War and closure of the Chanel Couture House. Of the five buildings in rue Cambon, only one stays open, the shop at number 31, where the perfumes and accessories continue to sell well.

1954   The great 'comeback'. Chanel returns to open 31, rue Cambon at the age of seventy-one. She launches her collection with a jersey suit, the 'No. 5'.

1955   Awarded the Fashion Oscar by Stanley Neiman Marcus, owner of the famous Neiman Marcus department stores in Dallas, to honour 'the most influential female designer of the twentieth century'. Launch of first eau de toilette for men, 'Pour Monsieur'.

1959   'No. 5' bottle exhibited at the Museum of Modern Art in New York.

1970   Launch of 'No. 19' perfume.

1971   Chanel dies 10 January. Her posthumous collection is a great success.

1974   Launch of 'Cristalle' perfume.

1975   Launch of the Chanel Beauty Collection of make-up and beauty products.

1978   Mass launch of the 'Chanel Boutique', offering ready-to-wear clothes and
        accessories. Today there are approximately sixty Chanel Boutiques around the world.

1981   Launch of the eau de toilette for men, 'Antaeus'.

1983   Karl Lagerfeld becomes Design Consultant in charge of Collections at the House
        of Chanel. Opening of a second Chanel Boutique in Paris at 42, avenue Montaigne.
        Relaunch of the perfumes 'Gardénia', 'Bois des Iles' and 'No. 22' exclusively at rue
        Cambon.

1984   Launch of the perfume 'Coco'.

1986   Chanel receives the Dé d'Or for the 1986 Autumn/Winter Haute Couture Collection
        created by Karl Lagerfeld. Launch of eau de parfum 'No. 5' as advertised by Carole
        Bouquet throughout the world.

1987   Le Temps Chanel (publicity campaign): launch of the Chanel watch 'Première', and
        opening of the first watch boutique in avenue Montaigne.

1988   Karl Lagerfeld and the House of Chanel win the Special Award for International
        Fashion presented by the Council of Fashion Designers of America (CFDA).

1989   Large exhibition devoted to Chanel for the opening of the Fashion and Costume
        section of the Musée des Arts Décoratifs in Marseilles.

1990   Launch of 'Egoiste', the eau de toilette for men. Launch of the watch
        'Mademoiselle' and opening of the watch and jewelry boutique in place Vendôme.

1993   Launch of Chanel jewelry and of 'Egoiste Platinum', eau de toilette for men.

1994   Launch of the 'Matellassée' watch and The Corps Actif line.

1995   Launch of a new look in make-up, 'Les Editions Ephémères'.

1996   Fashion show of the 1996 Haute Couture Spring/Summer Collection at the Ritz
        as a homage to Coco Chanel. Launch of the perfume 'Allure'.

Bibliography

Haedrich, Marcel, *Coco Chanel, Her Life, Her Secrets*. London and Boston, 1972.

Mauriès, Patrick, *Jewelry by Chanel*. Thames and Hudson, London, 1993.

Charles-Roux, Edmonde, *Chanel and her World*. Weidenfeld and Nicholson, London, 1981.

Charles-Roux, Edmonde, *Chanel*. Knopf, New York, 1975/Collins Harvill, London, 1989.

Morand, Paul, *L'Allure de Chanel*. Hermann, Paris, 1976.

Galante, Pierre, *Mademoiselle Chanel*. Chicago, 1973.

Delay, Claude, *Chanel solitaire*. London, 1973.

Leymarie, Jean, *Chanel*. Skira, Geneva, 1987.

Chanel

Chanel before Chanel. Even as a newcomer to early-twentieth-century Parisian society, Coco was creating a style that was all her own. Using soft flowing lines, her designs were stripped of all Belle Epoque affectations, as illustrated here by Karl Lagerfeld, 1991. © Chanel.

A stunning photograph of Coco from 1912, before she cut her hair. She is dressed up for a ball in the costume of a page boy at a village wedding. Her close-fitting jacket, black bow and round hat are pure Chanel. Private collection.

In the roaring twenties, when the garçonne look was all the rage, Coco Chanel clothed the first generation of liberated women. Karl Lagerfeld's drawings of 1991 show a few of the designs she invented which flew in the face of convention. © Chanel.

Coco and her friends were the couturière's first models and her designs were tailored to meet her own needs. She is shown here on board the 'Flying Cloud' with Marcelle Meyer, the pianist from the Les Six, c. 1928. Collection Boris Kochno.

During the thirties, Chanel bought 'La Pausa', a beautiful villa on the Côte d'Azur, where she spent the summer months swimming in the sea, sunbathing and relaxing. The look she created through this simple but refined way of life has still not dated. © Chanel.

Chanel in her English period, photographed here with her friend Vera Bates in 1928. Both had borrowed tweeds and sweaters belonging to Chanel's wealthy lover, the Duke of Westminster. She started a whole new fashion without meaning to. Private collection.

Chanel loved photographers. She was the first to make use of them not just to 'communicate' her fashions, but also to promote her own image. Photographed here by Horst at her home, Gabrielle is fifty years old and is at the height of her fame, power and beauty. Much more than just a visual record, the photograph conjures up an entire style in one image. This thirties style as visualized by Karl Lagerfeld in 1991 is shown *right*. © Horst P. Horst/R. J. Horst/ Hamiltons (left). © Chanel (right).

Comet brooch. In 1932 Chanel created a fabulous series of white jewelry in diamonds and platinum. © Photo Laziz Hamani, 1995.

Coco with Serge Lifar in Monte Carlo for the 1933 summer sporting season. Unlike most other fashion designers between the wars, Coco Chanel entertained in the same style as her clients. © Photo all rights reserved. SBM Archives.

For the 1987 Chanel Autumn/Winter Haute Couture Collection, Karl Lagerfeld designed this black velvet dress edged with white pearls, illustrated here by Ruben Alterio for *La Mode en peinture* (No. 12).

Androgynous, enigmatic and chic: the woman who set the fashion by appearing to ignore it. Shown here on holiday at the Venice Lido in 1936. Photograph by V. H. Grandpierre. © All rights reserved.

Tiny pearls were used to create this remarkable quilted evening dress designed by Karl Lagerfeld in 1990 with pearl embroidery by Lesage. The belt is made of engraved pâte-de-verre inspired by the Chinese. © Photo Keiichi Tahara, 1990.

The famous strings of fake pearls and the precious stones in ornamental settings of Byzantine inspiration. Created by Coco Chanel and produced by the House of Gripoux, they brightened up her little black dresses. © Photo Keiichi Tahara 1990.

A striking image of newfound freedom in a changing world. Coco is shown sitting on the shoulders of Serge Lifar, the star dancer at the time of the Ballets Russes. On holiday she appropriated men's fashions – note the cotton trousers and espadrilles – but she was never seen without her pearls. This look was recaptured by Karl Lagerfeld in his 1995 Haute Couture Collection, illustrated here by Mats Gustafson. © Mats Gustafson, A+C Anthology (right). Photo Jean Morain (left).

Descended from an old Sicilian family, the Duca di Verdura produced some of the most beautiful Chanel jewelry for the designer in the thirties, such as this cuff bracelet from 1930 made of ivory coloured lacquered metal inlaid with faceted crystals in different colours. Coco never abandoned this concept of 'sumptuous fakes', like this design from the sixties, even when Verdura went on to pursue his own brilliant career in New York. Lipnitski Foundation. © Roger-Viollet (left). Photo D. Genet, © Chanel (right).

The photographer Cecil Beaton, a friend of Chanel, shows her at home in the flat she was then renting on the ground floor of the Pillet-Will Hotel, rue du Faubourg Saint-Honoré (c. 1935). © Photo Cecil Beaton. Courtesy of Sotheby's, London.

The timeless Chanel style. After ten years' exile for wartime indiscretions, Chanel made her comeback when she was over seventy years old, setting a fashion for the active woman that would survive for generations to come: the little braid-trimmed suit, the quilted bag, the camellia, the lightweight dresses, visualized here by Karl Lagerfeld. © Chanel. And from 1956 (right), one of Chanel's most beautiful designs: a simple black suit lined in white satin. Photo Frances MacLaughlin, *Vogue*, Paris, March 1956. © All rights reserved.

The Chanel trademarks from the fifties onwards were collarless tweed suits, shantung silk blouses with turned-back cuffs, and thin gilt chains. Autumn/Winter Collection 1958. Photo Santo Forlano taken at rue Cambon. © *Vogue*, Paris September 1958.
One of the very first supermodels, Suzy Parker was for a long time the 'face' of Chanel. She is shown here wearing another great classic, the discreetly erotic calf-length dress in draped chiffon. Photo J. F. Clair, 1956. © Scoop/Elle.

Coco Chanel surrounded by her favourite things in the living room of her flat. She never slept here but used it merely as a meeting place where she received all of Paris during the fifties and sixties. Sitting on her famous beige suede sofa which she believed, in a sense rightly, to be the centre of the world, she would make witty or cutting remarks for the benefit of her select audience. She is pictured here with Jeanne Moreau, 1961. Photo by Giancarlo Botti. © Stills.

Coco and America. The most tragic and unwelcome publicity that a little Chanel suit was ever to receive: Jacqueline Kennedy after the assassination of her husband on 22 November 1963. © UP/Bettmann.
Marilyn Monroe. When in 1955 she was asked by journalists what she wore in bed, Monroe replied 'Chanel No.5', unwittingly inventing a slogan which swept the world. © Michael Ochs Archives, Ltd.

Although she refused to meet many of her clients, Coco Chanel always had time for the young and dazzlingly beautiful Romy Schneider. The film director Luchino Visconti asked his old friend to advise his newest star in her portrayal of a perverse and sophisticated Italian aristocrat in his film *Boccaccio 70* made in 1970. © Starfilms.

Chanel in the dressing room with her models. She liked to select young women from good families, whose deportment had to be as impeccable on the catwalk as it was off. She saw herself as a strict but helpful mother to these girls, introducing them to the highest spheres of international society. Photo Hatami, 1965. © Chanel.

The two-tone shoe. In the early sixties, Chanel had the idea of creating a shoe in two colours to make the foot look shorter. Produced by the shoemaker André Massaro, this slingback design with its many variations remains one of the most striking as well as the most famous symbols of the Chanel style. © Photo Laziz Hamani.

The great staircase at rue Cambon which led from the boutique to the haute couture salons and on to Chanel's apartment. Through the clever play of mirrors, Chanel could follow all that went on in her couture house from one floor, whether presiding over her fashion shows or checking the reactions of her customers. One such customer was Marlene Dietrich, shown here arriving for a show in the sixties holding one of the already coveted invitations. © Photo Assouline (left). © Photo all rights reserved (right).

The initially shy Coco, whose friends referred to her as 'the only active volcano in the Auvergne', managed to secure the friendship or at least the affection of some of the most brilliant personalities of the early twentieth century. As the only woman of her standing in a man's world, she liked to seduce them but without holding on to them. © Photo Roger Schall. © Lipnitzki Foundation, Roger Viollet.

Chanel in the nineties. Under Karl Lagerfeld, Chanel designs were more than ever at the forefront of fashion. The couturier is photographed here in private surrounded by the five models used in the 1995 Spring/Summer Haute Couture Collection. These strapless bodiced dresses with their organza flounces were inspired by Scarlett O'Hara, the heroine of *Gone with the Wind*. Photo Jean-Marie Perrier. © Scoop/Elle.

In the eighteenth-century setting of the couturier's private hotel, Karl Lagerfeld takes his own photographs of the two top models he likes to use to show off his designs. Linda Evangelista (left) and Christy Turlington (right) model two designs from the 1990-1991 Autumn/Winter Haute Couture Collection. Photo Karl Lagerfeld. © Chanel.

A tribute to the great lady of fashion. The model Stella Tennant wears a Chanel suit from the 1996 Spring/Summer Haute Couture Collection, photographed by Karl Lagerfeld in one of the suites at the Ritz where Chanel lived for more than thirty years. © Chanel.

The essence of Chanel in the details of a two-tone tweed suit from the 1993 Spring/Summer Haute Couture Collection. © Photo Laziz Hamani. © Chanel.

Tradition and innovation. The model Kristen McNemany photographed here by Karl Lagerfeld in one of the chic but shocking black and white tweed suits created for the 1991 Spring/Summer Haute Couture Collection. © Chanel.

Behind the scenes on two surprise visits to the renowned workshops at rue Cambon, where Karl Lagerfeld's designs are being carefully worked out following strict haute-couture rules. Photo Edouard Boubat, 1993.

Low-cut in leathers: Chanel in the nineties. Photographed by Peter Lindbergh in the streets of New York, supermodels pose in evening dresses and leather jackets. Karl Lagerfeld designed everything except the motorbikes and the oil-drums. Ready-to-Wear, Autumn/Winter 1991-1992. Photo Peter Lindbergh for article 'Wild at Heart' in *Vogue US*, New York, 1989.

Design for quilted bag. The indispensable accessory for the Chanel outfit, created in 1930. Photo Laziz Hamani, 1993. © Editions Assouline.

Haute couture, classicism and modernity: the marriage of the little Chanel suit with black leather. Shalom Harlow is photographed here by Karl Lagerfeld, holding the timeless quilted bag. Ready-to-Wear, Autumn/Winter 1995-1996. © Chanel.

This long dress in golden tulle and lace embroidered by François Lesage takes its inspiration from a design worn by Coco Chanel in 1937. Spring/Summer Haute Couture Collection 1996. © Chanel.

'The Chanel Classic Bottle No.5: the most treasured name in perfume'. Print by Andy Warhol, commissioned by Chanel perfumes. Silk-screen print on canvas. © Photo The Andy Warhol Foundation Inc. ARS. © ADAGP, Paris 1996.

Then and now: faces change, fashions come and go but style remains. On the left, the actress Marion Moorhouse wears a chiffon dress photographed by Edward Steichen. Courtesy of *Vogue* © 1928. On the right, nearly sixty years later, the model Shalom Harlow in a creation by Karl Lagerfeld for the Chanel 1996 Spring/Summer Haute Couture Collection. © Chanel.

Karl Lagerfeld drawn by himself. The Director of the Haute Couture and Ready-to-Wear Collections since 1983. Drawing by Karl Lagerfeld. © Chanel.

The timeless Gabrielle Chanel as photographed by Man Ray in 1935. No woman of today can wear her clothes with the same allure. © 1996, Man Ray Trust/ADAGP, Paris.

The publishers would like to thank the House of Chanel for the help they have given in the preparation of this work, in particular: Marie-Louise de Clermont-Tonnerre, Karl Lagerfeld, Jacques Helleu, Pierre Buntz, Patrick Doucet, Eric Pfrunder, Florence Mittnach-Rocher, Véronique Pérez, Véronique Depardieu, Catherine Cruse and Agathe Legall.

We also wish to thank all those who contributed to this work, in particular Madame Jeanne Moreau, Shalom Harlow, Linda Evangelista, Christy Turlington, Kristen McNemany, Cindy Crawford, Helena Christensen, Stephanie Seymour, Claudia Schiffer, Naomi Campbell, Nadja Auerman, Thera Matino, Olga Pantuschenkova, Tatiana Zavialova, Diane Heidkruger, Stella Tennant, Keiichi Tahara, Laziz Hamani, Ruben Alterio, André Massaro, Véronique Chaubin, Lydia Cresswell-Jones, Sabine Killinger, Cathy Queen and Nicole Chamson.